3-D THRILLERS!

T. REX
and Other Dangerous Dinosaurs

HEATHER AMERY & PAUL HARRISON

■SCHOLASTIC

New York • Toronto • London • Auckland
Sydney • Mexico City • New Delhi • Hong Kong

WHEN DINOSAURS

Millions of years before people lived on Earth, the world belonged to dinosaurs! These amazing creatures first appeared about 215 million years ago ("mya" for short) and ruled Earth for about 150 million years. Humans have only been around for 1.7 million years!

▲ Can you dig it?

When dinosaurs died, their bodies usually rotted away and nothing remained. But if a dinosaur died and the conditions were right, the bones would gradually *petrify* (turn to stone). By studying petrified remains, fossil experts, called *paleontologists*, can learn what dinosaurs were like.

Scientists believe there are HUNDREDS of dinosaur species yet to be found. So start DIGGING—the next big discovery may be YOURS!

Dinosaur days ▶

Dinosaurs first appeared during the Triassic Period (251–200 mya). One of the earliest dinosaurs was *Herrerasaurus* (heh-ray-rah-SORE-us). The Jurassic Period (200–145 mya) was dominated by plant eaters such as *Stegosaurus* (STEG-oh-SORE-us) and meat eaters such as *Allosaurus* (al-oh-SORE-us). And the Cretaceous Period (145–65 mya) saw the arrival of *Triceratops* (try-SER-a-tops).

DOMINATED

GENTLE GIANTS

The biggest creatures that ever walked Earth were the *herbivorous* (plant-eating) dinosaurs. *Seismosaurus* (SIZE-moh-SORE-us) may have measured nearly 130 feet (40 m). That's the length of two bowling alleys!

MAMENCHISAURUS's (mah-MEN-Key-SORE-us) neck measured 40 FEET (12 m) long—that's longer than a BUS!

◀ Vegetarian vengeance

Imagine a long-necked reptile the height of six men and as heavy as a dozen elephants! *Brachiosaurus* (brak-ee-oh-SORE-us) was too big to run or move quickly, but it had a thick and powerful tail, great for whacking hungry Jurassic attackers such as *Allosaurus* and *Ceratosaurus* (seh-rat-oh-SORE-us).

Tough love ▶

The plant-eating *Pachycephalosaurus* (PAK-ee-SEF-a-loh-SORE-us) had a huge dome of thick bone on the top of its skull. Some scientists believe that rival males would fight for females by charging at each other headfirst.

▼ Weapons or AC?

Paleontologists used to think that the plates on the back of a *Stegosaurus* were defense weapons. Now, most agree that they were a sort of prehistoric thermostat that helped warm or cool the dinosaur's body temperature.

MONSTER MEAT

Carnivorous (meat-eating) dinosaurs were fearsome! *Giganotosaurus* (JI-gah-NO-tuh-sore-us) was massive, while *Compsognathus* (komp-sog-NAY-thus) was about the same size as a chicken! But regardless of size, these carnivores all had ferocious teeth for ripping meat apart, and rows of razor-sharp claws!

When the leg bone of MEGALOSAURUS (MEG-ah-loh-SORE-us) was first found, people thought they had discovered the remains of a GIANT man!

▲ Run for your life!

Some of the most dangerous carnivores were small but speedy—and well armed! *Deinonychus* (DY-noh-NY-kus) was only 11 feet (3.4 m) long, but fast and fierce. Its name, which means "terrible claw," refers to the long, curved claw on each of its back feet, which it used to slash its prey.

EATERS

Food fights ▶

Some plant-eating dinosaurs may have been gentle, but they didn't necessarily give up without a struggle. In Mongolia's Gobi Desert, the bones of a meat-eating *Velociraptor* (vel-O-si-RAP-tor, meaning "speedy robber") and the bones of a plant-eating *Protoceratops* (pro-toe-SER-a-tops) were found together, indicating a fight to the finish.

▼ Armed and dangerous

At nearly 39 feet (12 m) long, *Allosaurus* was the top predator of the Jurassic Period. It had a powerful tail, three strong claws on each hand, and a mouthful of teeth with jagged edges perfect for tearing and chewing flesh.

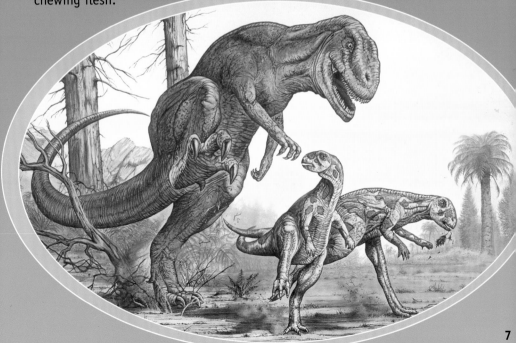

T. REX—TYRANT

One dinosaur stands out from all the rest—the famous *Tyrannosaurus rex* (tie-RAN-o-SORE-us rex), or *T. rex* for short. We know that *T. rex* lived in the Cretaceous Period, but what was this dinosaur really like? Was it as fearsome as we think? A lot of research has been done, but scientists are still trying to find the answers.

◀ Big boy

Tyrannosaurus rex lived in North America around 85 to 65 mya. It is also one of the biggest meat-eating dinosaurs ever discovered. It measured over 43 feet (13 m) from nose to tail, and when it stretched up, *T. rex* could reach up to 20 feet (6 m) high. It weighed between 5 and 8 tons (4.5 and 7 t), which means it was heavier than an elephant.

KING

▲ Tall Tail

T. rex had a stiff, pointed tail that stuck out at the back. This heavy tail probably acted as a counterweight to its huge head, giving the dinosaur greater balance and agility—particularly useful when making sharp turns and chasing lunch!

◄ Changing world

T. rex lived at the end of the dinosaurs' reign. During the Cretaceous Period, the shapes of the continents were very different. Most of the land was in two large masses called Gondwana and Laurasia. By the time *T. rex* appeared, these landmasses had broken up and started to form the continents we know today.

FEARSOME FIND

Around 30 *T. rex* skeletons have been discovered, and not all of these are in good condition or anywhere near complete. For these reasons, a good specimen attracts a lot of attention.

▶ Fossil hunters

The very first *T. rex* fossil was discovered by Barnum Brown in 1902. Today, paleontologists like Jack Horner, right, are continuing his work. Jack discovered *Maiasaura* (MY-ah-sore-uh) and was the first person to realize that some dinosaurs cared for their young.

◀ Femme fatale

The most famous *Tyrannosaurus rex* of all is in The Field Museum in Chicago. She was named Sue after the woman who found her—Sue Hendrickson. Discovered in South Dakota, Sue is one of the most complete skeletons of a *T. rex* ever found, and also the largest. The skeleton was so well preserved, it helped paleontologists learn a great deal about these huge dinosaurs.

▼ Moving monster

Improvements in robotics mean that moving, or *animatronic*, models are popular at visitor attractions. Visitors to museums such as London's Natural History Museum can get close to a ferocious, roaring *T. rex*—but luckily this is as close as we'll ever get to being face-to-face with a real one.

The name *Tyrannosaurus rex* means "TYRANT LIZARD KING." Wow, that's scary!

GETTING TO THE

Without a doubt, it's *Tyrannosaurus rex*'s fearsome head that makes it such a scary and impressive specimen. At around 5 feet (1.5 m) long, its skull was as big as your average 12-year-old kid, and was packed full of dangerous teeth!

▼ Mouthful of misery

If you were unfortunate enough to see inside a *T. rex*'s mouth, you would find about 60 razor-sharp teeth. Some measured up to 12 inches (30.5 cm) long, and they curved backward. This meant that when the dinosaur bit its victim, it couldn't get away!

POINT

Big bite ▶

T. rex's mouth was big enough to swallow a human whole, so it's no surprise that such a big mouth could give a massive bite. Scientists have worked out that a T. rex could easily chomp its way through thick dinosaur bones.

▲ Small arms

One question still puzzles paleontologists—what were T. rex's arms for? They were so small they couldn't reach its mouth, and would have been useless for picking things up since they only had two claws at the end. However, its claws were really sharp, and its arms were very strong—perhaps they were for pushing the dinosaur off the ground? A puzzling, if short, mystery!

T. REX was always growing new TEETH, so when an old one fell out or got KNOCKED out, a new one was ready to replace it!

A SAVAGER OR

Everyone agrees that *Tyrannosaurus rex* was the supercarnivore of its time. But what paleontologists can't agree on is whether this fearsome-looking dinosaur hunted for food or was a *scavenger*.

▶ Dead or alive?

Animals that scavenge eat animals that have died or been killed, instead of hunting for live prey. It may be that *T. rex* took the easy option when it came to eating.

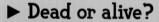

◀ The nose knows

Paleontologists who argue that *T. rex* was a scavenger say that it had a good sense of smell. Scavengers, such as vultures, can smell rotting meat from far away. But maybe *T. rex* used its sense of smell for tracking live prey?

SCAVENGER?

Eye can see you ▶

One of the strongest arguments in favor of *T. rex* being a hunter rather than a scavenger is the position of its eyes. The eyes face forward, like a human's, rather than to the sides, like a horse's. Forward-facing eyes give a better sense of where objects are, which is why predators such as tigers have eyes in this position.

Slowpoke

One thing's for sure, *T. rex* was no speed freak. After studying its leg bones and muscles, scientists believe this dinosaur had a top speed of about 25 miles per hour (40 kph)—faster than an average human, but pretty slow when compared to many dinosaurs. Plus, it seems that *T. rex* could only keep up this speed for a short sprint.

TYRANNOSAURUS:

When you hear the word *dinosaur*, what springs to mind? *T. rex*—king of the dinosaurs? The "rex" part of its name means "king," but does *T. rex* still hold the title? Not anymore— paleontologists have unearthed even bigger meat eaters!

King lizard ▶

T. rex belongs to a family of dinosaurs known as tyrannosaurs. *Albertosaurus* (al-BER-toe-SORE-us) was slightly smaller but very similar to *T. rex*. Several fairly complete skeletons have been found, many in the Canadian province of Alberta, after which this dinosaur is named. But *T. rex* is still the tallest and heaviest tyrannosaur.

THE EX-REX?

▼ Heads—you win!

In 2006 Montana State University unveiled a *T. rex* skull, originally unearthed in the 1960s. Now reconstructed, the skull measures 59 inches (150 cm) long—beating that of Sue at The Field Museum in Chicago (see page 10) by at least 3.5 inches (9 cm).

New King on the block ▶

Giganotosaurus, whose name means "giant lizard of the south," was discovered in Argentina in 1993. Its skull and thigh bones are bigger than Sue's. Then, in the late 1990s, *Carcharodontosaurus* (kar-CHA-row-DON-toe-SORE-us) was found. Although a complete skeleton hasn't been discovered, scientists think it could be even bigger than *Giganotosaurus.*

OFF TO A FLYING

What was life like for a baby *Tyrannosaurus rex*? The Cretaceous forest was a dangerous place for a juvenile, who could be crushed by large plant-eating dinosaurs or eaten by other meat eaters. It could even be eaten by one of its parents!

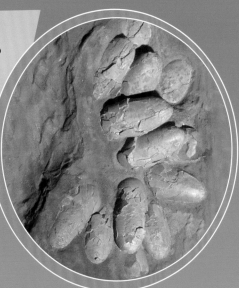

▲ Eggs

Like all dinosaurs, a baby *T. rex* began life as an egg. So far, no tyrannosaur eggs have been discovered, so we don't know what they looked like. They may have been long and thin, like these *Protoceratops* eggs found in Mongolia.

◄ Surprise!

Crocodile parents cover their eggs with leaves or earth to keep them warm so that the babies will hatch. Perhaps *T. rex* parents did the same with their eggs?

START

Feathered friend ►

Many scientists think that birds descended from dinosaurs. This fossilized *Sinornithosaurus* (SI-nor-ni-tho-SORE-us) found in China had feathers. Some baby dinosaurs may have had feathers, too, to keep them warm.

Some scientists think all dinosaurs had feathers. Imagine T. REX as a HUGE, ferocious CHICKEN!

► Thanks, Mom!

Fossils show that certain dinosaurs may have protected their young. Paleontologists think that *Maiasaura*, or "good mother lizard," fed its young in the nest until they were old enough to move out into the open.

THE CREATURES

While dinosaurs roamed Earth, awesome beasts ruled the seas. Many of them adapted to life in the water, coming to the surface to breathe, like whales today. Prehistoric sea monsters came in all shapes and sizes. One of the biggest, *Kronosaurus* (KRON-oh-sore-us), had a 9-foot (2.7 m) head!

Well-preserved FOSSILS suggest that ichthyosaurs didn't lay EGGS but instead gave birth to LIVE babies in the water!

▼ Gone fishin'

Ichthyosaurs (IKH-thee-oh-sores) were the superswimmers of the prehistoric seas. With their sleek bodies, back flippers, and strong tails, icthyosaurs looked a lot like dolphins—but they were *much* bigger. This *Shonisaurus* (shon-ee-SORE-us) was 50 feet (15 m) long!

▼ Rock bottom

With extralong necks and fat bodies, the group of sea reptiles known as plesiosaurs (ple-SEE-oh-sores) may have looked awkward, but they swam just fine, thanks to paddle-like flippers that helped them twist and turn.

► Monster or myth?

The most famous sea monster is Scotland's "Nessie," the so-called Loch Ness Monster. Descriptions of a huge creature in the lake make it sound as if Nessie could be a modern-day plesiosaur. But few people believe such monsters exist today.

21

FLYING REPTILES

In prehistoric times, flying reptiles called pterosaurs (TEH-ruh-sores) ruled the skies. Some were as tiny as a sparrow, but others had the wingspan of a small plane!

▼ Superscooper

Pteranodon (ter-RAN-oh-don) had a pointy crest on its head and even pointier jaws. *Pteranodon* would skim through the water, scoop up fish, and swallow them whole—just as pelicans do today.

AIR-volution ▶

Rhamphorhynchus
(RAM-foh-RING-khus),
an early pterosaur, had
spiky teeth for spearing
fish. It also had a long
tail with a kite-shaped
piece of skin on the
end that may have
helped it to steer.
Later flying reptiles
such as *Quetzalcoatlus*
(kwet-zal-co-AT-lus)
had shorter tails but
longer necks.

And finally—feathers! ▶

Archaeopteryx (ar-kee-OP-ter-iks) is
the first flying creature known to
have had feathers. But don't let
that fool you—this was no bird.
Its fossils reveal the skeleton
of a reptile with dinosaur-like
teeth and claws on its wings,
which it may have used to climb
trees. Scientists think it may
have glided rather than flown.
It is seen as a link between the
dinosaurs and modern-day birds.

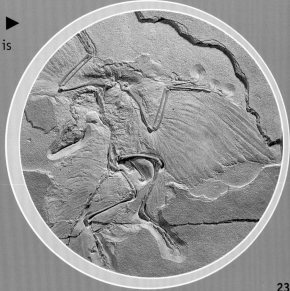

ASTEROID!

The dinosaurs ruled for 150 million years. But 65 mya, they all disappeared. What happened? Did something kill them, or did they gradually die out? One theory is that a giant asteroid crashed into Earth, with catastrophic results.

▼ There goes the neighborhood

An asteroid collision would have thrown up huge clouds of dust and blocked out the sun for weeks or months. Many small animals (such as mammals, birds, and insects) would have survived. But reptiles would have frozen or starved to death without the sun.

Lights out ▶

It would have taken a massive asteroid to plunge the planet into darkness. And it would have left a mighty big hole! Such a hole does exist; it's called the Chicxulub crater, and it's off Mexico's Yucatán Peninsula. Most of the crater is covered by the sea, but we now know that it is nearly 112 miles (180 km) across. That's a big dent!

About 65 mya the dinosaurs, pterosaurs, AND the sea reptiles all disappeared. No more GIANT reptiles to dominate the planet!

Crossing the boundary

To make a hole as big as Chicxulub, the asteroid would have been about 6 miles (9.5 km) across. Debris scattered by an enormous asteroid impact has been found all around the world and can be seen as a layer in the rocks that paleontologists call the K–T boundary. Below this line you can find dinosaur fossils, but above the line—nothing.

THE DINOSAURS

Apart from the giant asteroid idea, there are several other theories that try to explain why the dinosaurs disappeared.

Violent volcanoes ▶

One theory suggests that huge volcanoes spewed so much lava, volcanic ash, and poisonous gas into the air that it caused the climate to cool down. Maybe the dinosaurs couldn't survive the change in climate and died out?

▼ Wild ideas

Another wild theory claims that mammals may have eaten all the dinosaur eggs—but that's a lot of eggs for tiny mammals to eat! A less dramatic explanation is that the climate changed and gradually life on Earth changed, too. Once warm and tropical, the weather became drier and cooler, which was fine for some animals, but devastating for dinosaurs, who couldn't handle the big chill.

DISAPPEAR

ANSWERS FROM

E verything we know about dinosaurs comes from the painstaking work of fossil hunters, paleontologists, and other scientists. Fossils are scanned, magnified, and X-rayed in an effort to find out as much as possible about what dinosaurs looked like and how they lived.

The only way PALEONTOLOGISTS will find out more about dinosaurs is by finding more FOSSILS. So get HUNTING!

Color question ▶

Fossils can tell us a lot, but they can't tell us what color dinosaurs were. Scientists look at today's animals for clues. Hunters, such as lions, aren't bright pink, since they would be spotted a mile away. Instead they are a dull color to blend into the background. Perhaps the same was true for dinosaurs?

THE PAST

▼ Warm or cold?

Another question puzzling paleontologists is whether dinosaurs were warm- or cold-blooded. Mammals, such as tigers, are *warm-blooded*—their bodies are ready to move as soon as they wake up. Reptiles are *cold-blooded*—they need to warm up in the sun first. Dinosaurs were reptiles, so they may have been cold-blooded. Birds, however, which probably evolved from dinosaurs, are warm-blooded. So who knows the answer?

Dirty business ▶

Being a paleontologist isn't always very glamorous, especially if your job is inspecting dinosaur poo! Fossilized poo is called *coprolite*. It can tell paleontologists a lot about what dinosaurs ate.

THRILLER FACTS

Now that you've walked with the dinosaurs, maybe you think you know it all? Well, here are a few more amazing facts to make you into a real dinosaur expert!

▼ Sound of silence

Although fossils can tell us plenty about what the dinosaurs were like, there is one important thing that paleontologists just don't know—what did the dinosaurs actually sound like? Did *T. rex* roar, squeak, cluck, hiss, or bark?

Dinosaur skin

Paleontologists have discovered the remains of dinosaur skin! Evidence suggests that dinosaurs had skin similar to modern-day crocodiles.

▲ Kings of the sea

Long-necked plesiosaurs were huge, measuring up to 40 feet (12 m) in length. But their short-necked relatives, the pliosaurs (PLY-oh-sores), were even longer. In Mexico in 2002, an enormous pliosaur, the Monster of Aramberri, was discovered. It was roughly 50 feet (15 m) long—about the same as eight men lying head to foot!

Some plant-eating dinosaurs swallowed polished PEBBLES, perhaps to help GRIND UP a leafy lunch in their stomachs!

Monster record

In the UK in 2009, a new discovery was unveiled—the head of a pliosaur that could be the largest on record. The animal is estimated to have been over 52 feet (16 m) long!

This edition created in 2010 by
Arcturus Publishing Limited, 26/27 Bickels Yard,
151–153 Bermondsey Street, London SE1 3HA

ISBN 978-0-545-21848-1

10 9 8 7 6 5 4 3 2 1   10 11 12 13 14

Printed in Malaysia 106

First Scholastic edition, June 2010

ARCTURUS CREDITS
Authors: Heather Amery and Paul Harrison
Editors: Jacqueline McCann and Lisa Miles
Designers: Beatrice Reis Custodio and Mike Reynolds
Illustrator (glasses): Ian Thompson

PICTURE CREDITS
Ardea: p. 2, p. 21 bottom, p. 22, p. 23 bottom
Discovery Communications Inc: p. 21 top,
   p. 23 top
Jon Hughes/pixelshack.com: back cover left
Natural History Museum: front cover, p. 3,
   p. 4, p. 5 top and bottom, p. 6, p. 7 top and
   bottom, p. 8, p. 10 top, p. 11, p. 13 top and
   middle, p. 14 top, p. 15, p. 16, p. 17 top
   and bottom, p. 19 top and bottom, p. 20,
   p. 25, p. 26, p. 29 bottom, p. 30, p. 31,
   back cover right

Nature Picture Library/Anup Shah: p. 18 bottom
Oxford Scientific (OSF)/Photolibrary.com: p. 27
Science Photo Library: title page, p. 9 top and
   bottom, p. 12, p. 14 bottom, p. 18 top,
   p. 24, p. 28, p. 29 top
The Field Museum, Chicago: p. 10 bottom
   (GN89671_53c: John Weinstein)

3-D images produced by Pinsharp